WEXFORD

WEXFORD

Town of Heritage

Pat Dargan

EASTWOOD BOOKS

First published 2023 by Eastwood Books
Dublin, Ireland
www.eastwoodbooks.com
www.wordwellbooks.com

1

Eastwood Books is an imprint of the Wordwell Group.

The Wordwell Group is a member of Publishing Ireland,
the Irish Publishers' Association.

Eastwood Books
The Wordwell Group
Unit 9, 78 Furze Road
Sandyford
Dublin, Ireland

© Pat Dargan, 2023

ISBN: 978-1-913934-45-3 (Trade Paperback)

The right of Pat Dargan to be identified as the Author
of this work has been asserted in accordance with the
Copyright, Designs and Patents Act 1988.

All rights reserved. No part of this book may be reprinted
or reproduced or utilised in any form or by any electronic,
mechanical or other means, now known or hereafter invented,
including photocopying and recording, or in any information
storage or retrieval system, without the permission in writing
from the Publishers.

British Library Cataloguing in Publication Data.
A catalogue record for this book is available from the National Library of Ireland and
the British Library.

Typesetting and design by the Wordwell Group
Copyediting by Heidi Houlihan
Printed in Ireland by Sprint Print, Dublin

Contents

Previous published works by the author   7
List of Buildings   9
Diagrammatic Map of Wexford   11

Introduction   13

Medieval Wexford   15
Georgian Wexford   23
Victorian Wexford   53
Twentieth and Twenty-First-Century Wexford   89

Previous published works by the author

Exploring Georgian Dublin, 2008
Exploring Ireland's Historic Towns, 2010
Exploring Irish Castles, 2011
Exploring Celtic Ireland, 2011
Exploring Georgian Limerick, 2012
Georgian Bath, 2012
Georgian London – the West End, 2012
The Georgian Town House, 2013
Edinburgh New Town, co-authored by Carley, Dalziel and Laird, 2015
Dublin in 50 Buildings, 2017
Bath in 50 Buildings, 2018
Dublin Pubs, 2018
Limerick in 50 Buildings, 2019
Kilkenny – City of Heritage, 2020
Whitehaven in 50 Buildings, 2021

List of Buildings

1. St Peter and St Paul Church, Selskar Abbey, Temperance Row
2. Circular Wall Tower, George's Street Upper
3. Square Wall Tower, John's Gate Street
4. West Gate, Selskar Abbey, Temperance Row
5. St Patrick's Church, Patrick's Square
6. St Mary's Church, Mary's Lane
7. Terraced Town House, Abbey Street
8. Slate-fronted Town House, Allen Street
9. House and Shop, Main Street South
10. Town House, George's Street Lower
11. House and Shop, Main Street Lower
12. Corner House and Pub, Main Street Lower
13. Church of St Iberius, Main Street North
14. Former Market House, Corn Market
15. Terraced Town House, Abbey Street
16. Corner House and Pub, Bull Ring
17. Warehouse, Sinnot Place
18. Former Malt House, Peter Street
19. Mirrored House, Mary Street
20. Former Malt House, Peter Street
21. Former Bank, Crescent Quay
22. Harbour Office, Crescent Quay
23. Young Men's Christian Association Building, Main Street South
24. Former Methodist Church, Rowe Street Lower
25. United Presbyterian and Methodist Church, Anne Street
26. Former Granary, Charlotte Street
27. Church of the Immaculate Conception, John Street Lower

28. Mechanics Institute, Main Street North
29, Former Church of St Selskar, Selskar Abbey
30. Former Bank, Custom House Quay
31. Market Building, Bull Ring Square
32. Commercial Premises Building, Commercial Quay
32. Former Coffee House, Common Quay
33. Terraced House, Clifford Street
34, Former Temperance Coffee House, Common Quay Street
35. Corner House, George's Street Upper
36. Former Bank, Custom House Quay
37. Semi-detached House, Crescent Quay
38. Railway Station, Redmond Square
39. Office Building, Selskar Street
40. Post Office, Anne Street
41. House and Shop, Main Street South
42. Dormer Cottage, Slaney Street
43. Former Bakery, Main Street North
44. Bank Building, Main Street
45. Wexford Town Library, Mallin Street

Opposite page: Diagrammatic map of the historic core of Wexford with the position of the selected buildings indicated.

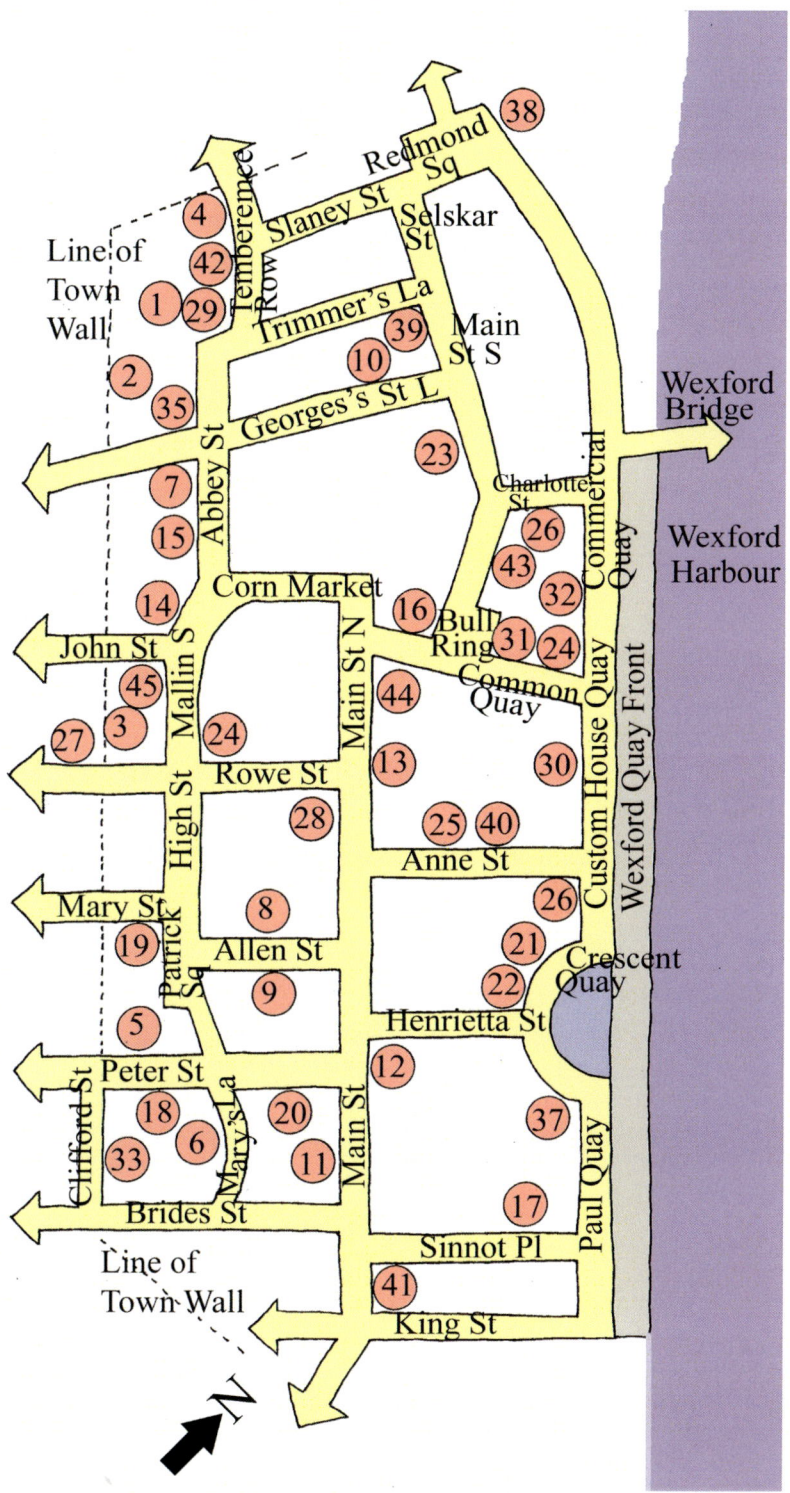

Introduction

The form of Wexford town has been shaped by four major spatial influences: Gaelic, Norman, Georgian, and Victorian. This has resulted in a rich body of historic buildings that form the focus of this work. The origins of the town, that lies around 130 kilometres south of Dublin, can be traced to Selskar Abbey, an early medieval monastic settlement positioned on the east bank of the wide estuary of the River Slaney. South of the monastery was a little stream that flowed eastwards into a deep pool and then into the estuary; and it was near this pool, now the Crescent Quay, that the Vikings established a raiding and trading station in the ninth century. The extent of the Viking settlement is uncertain, but it was probably positioned around South Main Street – although no trace of it remains above ground level.

In 1169 the area came under the control of the Normans and they proceeded to establish their presence. They built a castle, or fort, well to the south of the abbey, and around the thirteenth century began to lay out a new town in the form of two roughly parallel streets stretching northwards between the castle and the abbey, to which a number of irregular cross streets were added. This was followed by the building of a stone town wall on the landward side of the settlement with town gates and wall towers, although buildings fronting the riverside were left undefended, perhaps relying on the harbour as a natural moat. The result was the establishment of a linear walled town with the abbey at one end and the castle at the other with a pattern of narrow medieval streets. This pattern survives to the present day, acting as the historic core of the town, and includes an impressive display of medieval structures including: the remains of three churches, sections of the town wall, three defence towers, a town gate and a tower house.

During the eighteenth and nineteenth centuries most of the medieval buildings in the historic core of the town were removed and replaced by Georgian and subsequent Victorian building works. The same period saw the town castle replaced by a military barracks and an impressive bridge was built spanning the Slaney estuary. This provided a link between the historic core and Ferrybank on the far bank of the estuary. A new extensive riverside quay was also laid in place along the bank of the historic core – effectively establishing Wexford harbour. The town evolved into a prosperous industrial, trading town and seaport with a range of industrial, commercial and fishing enterprises and the town fabric extended well beyond the line of the medieval walls. The subsequent twentieth century saw little new development of the town's morphology except for the replacement of older buildings with new structures. An outstanding marine feature of the town was, however, the development of the new Quay Front along the harbour line that was completed in 2000. This stretches southwards between Wexford Bridge as far as King Street and successfully doubles as a wharf and dramatic landscaped pedestrian plaza. Today Wexford's historic core presents a vibrant and attractive built heritage of narrow streetscapes and urban architecture, which this volume explores. Here the individual buildings are presented in the order in which they were built, reflecting the physical character of Wexford's historic form.

Medieval Wexford

Twelfth to Thirteenth Centuries

1. St Peter and St Paul Church, Selskar Abbey, Twelfth Century

The Abbey of St Selskar is the oldest of Wexford's Gothic buildings and is located on Temperance Row in the north-east corner of the medieval sector of the town. It is thought to date from the twelfth century and was established by the Roche family as an Augustinian priory dedicated to St Peter and St Paul, within which the remains of three medieval elements partially survive. These include the ruins of the thirteenth-century church, the medieval church tower and the West Gate, which include a mixture of characteristic Gothic elements including: heavy masonry walling, pointed and arched door and window openings, and steep gables. In addition, the site holds the ruins of the nineteenth-century parish church (Building 29). The abbey was suppressed in 1541 during the Reformation, but remained in use for some time as a parish church. Little of the thirteenth-century double-nave church survives except for parts of the south and east walls including the remains of the west windows (Fig. 1) and the four pointed arches that separated the aisles (Fig. 2). During the fifteenth century a three-storey church tower was added to the south-east corner of the nave (Fig. 3). This was given a projecting corner stair tower and battlements. The stair tower extends a further level above the main block and is lit by narrow slit windows, while the main body of the tower has a number of round-headed windows. An interesting feature of the tower is the pair of carved heads set high upon the west wall, that may well date from an earlier ninth- or tenth-century period as well as a grave slab inserted near the base of the tower (Fig. 4).

Fig. 1. The surviving remnants of gables and pointed arched window openings of St Peter and St Paul Church, Selskar Abbey.

Fig. 2. The dividing arched arcade that separates the two aisles at St Peter and St Paul Church, Selskar Abbey.

Fig. 3. The tall square medieval church tower attached to St Peter and St Paul Church, Selskar Abbey.

Fig. 4. Grave slab embedded in the masonry of St Peter and St Paul Church tower, Selskar Abbey.

2. Circular Wall Tower, George's Street Upper, Twelfth Century

Following the taking of the town by the Normans towards the close of the twelfth century, work started on building the town wall and it was completed by around 1300. The southern line of the wall, of which little survives, stretched inland from the shoreline of Wexford harbour south of King Street and turned westwards at an angle as far as Clifford Street. The Norman town castle was erected just outside the wall at King Street, but this was demolished during the eighteenth century to make way for a military barracks. From Clifford Street, the wall follows a north-west course as far as Selskar Abbey, a distance of over a kilometre, from where it turned eastwards towards the shore. About two thirds of the wall survives along this north-west line including three wall towers, but little survives of the eastwards stretch. A short section of the eastern town wall can be accessed from George's Street Upper and stands about three metres high. This section also features a round tower that faces onto a green area (Fig. 5). The tower has a number of slit windows on the outer face around half way up, above which the tower has been restored and a stepped battlement added (Fig. 6).

Fig. 5. The circular wall tower, George's Street Upper.

Fig. 6. The slit window of the circular wall tower, George's Street Upper.

3. Square Wall Tower, John's Gate Street, Twelfth Century

Stretching south-east from St John's Gate Street is a further stretch of the town wall that faces onto the grounds of the Church of the Immaculate Conception (Fig. 7) which can also be accessed from the rear of the County Library building on Mallin Street. Here the stone wall tower is square in form with stone steps providing access to the high-level doorway, an arched recess on the town side (Fig. 8) and restored single-stepped battlements at roof level.

Fig. 7. The square wall tower and part of the town wall, John's Gate Street.

Fig. 8. The access steps, recessed base and battlements of the square wall tower.

4. West Gate, Selskar Abbey, Temperance Row, Thirteenth Century

The West Gate, also called Selskar Gate, on the east side of the town wall was completed during the thirteenth century (Fig. 9). This is the only surviving example of the town's original six gates. The others were demolished during the nineteenth century to improve the vehicular access into the town. The West Gate acted solely as a gate to Selskar Abbey and was not one of the formal town gates; hence, it survived the removal of the other gates. The four-storey tower is square in plan and sits within the town wall with a stair turret in the north-west corner. The entrance passage is barrel vaulted (Fig. 10). Immediately overhead is a round-headed window above which is a number of smaller windows. There is a projecting bartizan or gallery at the top level. This is positioned directly above the entrance archway and allowed defenders to direct their fire on attackers below. The roof level of the tower has a restored system of stepped battlements. From inside the gateway, the blocked-up outline of an arched pedestrian gateway can be noticed (Fig. 11).

Above: Fig. 9. The restored West Gate with its entrance arch and battlements, Selskar Abbey.

Above right: Fig. 10. The arched and vaulted West Gate, Selskar Abbey.

Right: Fig. 11. The blocked-up side gate to West Gate, Selskar Abbey.

5. St Patrick's Church, Patrick's Square, c. Thirteenth Century

During the medieval period Wexford town had five parish churches within the town wall, of which the ruins of two survive: St Patrick's and St Mary's. In addition, there were a further six churches immediately outside the wall – none of which survive. Entered from Patrick's Square on High Street, St Patrick's is the best preserved of the town's medieval churches. Nothing survives of the roof although most of the walling is intact (Fig. 12). The church dates from around the thirteenth century. It had a double nave with a four-pointed Gothic arched arcade dividing the two (Fig. 13). The interior of the church is divided into a chancel, where the altar was once positioned. It also features a nave and a wide Gothic chancel arch, the remains of a triple-arched window and a double-arched bellcote high up on the east gable (Fig. 14).

Above left: Fig. 12. The surviving walls and end gables, St Patrick's Church, Patrick's Square.

Left: Fig. 13. The dividing arcade and end gable, St Patrick's Church, Patrick's Square.

Above right: Fig. 14. The end gable, part of the triple window and double-arched bellcote of St Patrick's Church, Patrick's Square.

6. St Mary's Church, Mary's Lane, Thirteenth Century

St Mary's Church on Mary's Lane dates from around the thirteenth century although little of the fabric survives. The curved boundary on the eastern side of the churchyard suggests that the initial foundation was established around the ninth century. Today only part of the gable and part of a side wall of the nave remain standing (Fig. 15) with the outline of the rest of the double nave identifiable on the ground. A 1793 print of the interior shows the church in ruins, but offers a clear impression of how the church looked at that stage (Fig. 16). This includes a semi-circular chancel arch, a Gothic arched arcade, a double ogee window, and a double-arched bellcote on the gable.

Fig. 15. The surviving gable and portion of side wall, St Mary's Church, Mary's Lane.

Fig. 16. This 1793 print of St Mary's Church was drawn by John James Barralet and published in *The Antiques of Ireland*, published by M. Hooper.

Georgian Wexford

Eighteenth and Nineteenth Centuries

7. Terraced Town House, Abbey Street, *c.* Eighteenth Century

During the eighteenth and nineteenth centuries, the streetscape of Wexford underwent extensive redevelopment as the medieval houses and buildings were removed and gradually replaced by uniform Georgian terraced houses and buildings were laid out in narrow plots that opened directly onto the streets – a spatial arrangement that still forms the main framework and character of Wexford's historic core. The stone-built three-storey terraced town house on Abbey Street offers an excellent example of a Wexford Georgian town house. Externally it is rendered, ruled and lined to imitate cut stonework (Fig. 17), while internally the narrow house has a room to the front and a room to the rear, with the entrance hall and stairs positioned to one side. A characteristic feature of the house, and most Georgian houses of the period, is the gradual reduction of the floor to ceiling heights between the different floor levels. The lower rooms have the highest ceilings with lower ceiling heights on the upper floors. The house front at ground level has a pair of Georgian windows and a door case to one side, with the three windows on each of the upper floors spaced equally across the front. The arched door case is set into a moulded and arched surround with a panelled door, a rounded fanlight and panelled side columns (Fig. 18). The standard vertically proportioned timber Georgian windows have up-and-down sliding sashes with small glazing panes (Fig. 19). These reduce in height on each floor level to reflect the internal variations in floor to ceiling heights.

Fig. 17. The three-storey rendered terraced town house on Abbey Street has an arrangement of Georgian windows and the entrance door positioned to one side.

Fig. 18. The round-headed door case of the town house on Abbey Street has a panelled door and side columns with a rounded fanlight and moulded surrounds.

Fig. 19. The characteristic vertically proportioned timber Georgian windows of the house on Abbey Street have up-and-down sliding sashes with small glazing panes.

8. Slate-fronted Town House, Allen Street, c. Eighteenth Century

The house on Allen Street is part of a short terrace and is three storeys high over a basement, with a slate-hung front on the two upper levels (Fig. 20). This type of wall-hung slating is a feature of several eighteenth-century buildings in Wexford. The plain rendered ground-floor level of the house has a pair of characteristic vertically proportioned Georgian sliding sashes and a panelled door with a low rectangular fanlight to one side. Meanwhile, overhead the first- and second-floor levels have three standard Georgian sashes spaced equally across the front (Fig. 21). The basement level is below ground with the tops of the windows projecting just a little above the footpath level. Internally the original joinery, plasterwork and fireplaces remain intact.

Above: Fig. 20. The house on Allen Street has a slated front on the two upper levels and Georgian sliding sash windows on the three levels above the basement.

Right: Fig. 21. The Georgian sliding sash upper-floor window of the slate-fronted house on Allen Street has nine small glazing panes in contrast to the twelve panes of the partially replaced windows of the lower levels.

9. House and Shop, Selskar St, Ferrybank South, Nineteenth Century

The double-storey terraced house and shop on Selskar St dates from around 1850. The plain rendered elevation has an inserted shop front at ground level, Georgian windows spaced across the first-floor level, a slated roof, and an attic dormer window (Fig. 22). The elegant timber shop front has the shop door to one side and a wide display window divided into three panes by arched and moulded framing (Fig. 23). The moulded fascia that stretches across the front of the building has scrolled-end brackets and carries a painted shop sign. The upper floor has two Georgian-style windows with large panes, while overhead, the slated attic dormer window sits into the slated roof.

Left: Fig. 22. The three-storey house and shop is part of the Selskar St terraced streetscape.

Right: Fig. 23. The attractive inserted shop front of the house and shop on Selskar St has a wide door, a triple-arched display window and a titled, moulded and end-bracketed fascia.

10 Town House, George's Street Lower, Eighteenth Century

The town house is positioned at the end of a terrace in the only example of a Wexford street where the bulk of the Georgian streetscape remains intact (Fig. 24). The plain rendered narrow house is three storeys with a basement and a single Venetian-style window on each floor (Fig. 25). The Venetian window differs from the standard Georgian window in that it is placed in a square window opening, in contrast to the more common vertically proportioned opening, and includes a central sliding sash flanked on either side by slimmer sashes – in order to give the opening a Georgian vertical emphasis (Fig. 26). The two small standard Georgian windows at basement level are more Georgian in tradition and overlook a small low-level basement area. This is below the street level and screened from the footpath by a metal railing that stretches across the front of the house and returns up the stone steps to the door. The entrance doorway is set to one side and is reached by five cut-stone steps and the four-panelled door and the overhead shallow fanlight is set back a little from a moulded surround. An unusual surviving element of the Georgian period is the cast-iron boot scraper immediately outside the door (Fig. 27). This allowed the owner or visitors to scrape their boots and shoes before entering the house. Internally a number of the original timber and plasterwork elements survive.

Fig. 24. George's Street Lower is the only Wexford street where the Georgian character and atmosphere of the eighteenth-century residential streetscape survives mainly intact.

Left: Fig. 25. The tripartite Venetian windows and front railings are a notable feature of the narrow three-storey terraced town house on George's Street Lower.

Below left: Fig. 26. The tripartite Venetian windows of the narrow terraced house on George's Street Lower have a combination of a central sliding sash flanked by slim side sashes.

Below right: Fig. 27. The cast-iron foot scraper outside the door of the narrow terraced house on George's Street Lower is a rare surviving Wexford example of an interesting domestic feature.

11. House and Shop, 43 South Main Street, Eighteenth Century

The three-storey house and shop on South Main Street is one of an identical pair that dates from the eighteenth century (Fig. 28). It is one of the many houses where the ground floor was altered for retail use as Wexford town developed into a successful trading centre. These changes are particularly characteristic of the main shopping streets such as South Main Street. These changes from residential to retail were achieved by enlarging the ground-floor window openings of the original houses to create wide shop display windows, while retaining the doorway at one side to provide access to the upper-floor accommodation, which initially remained in residential and later commercial and office use. The timber shop front on the South Main Street premises has a traditional-style design that replaced an earlier shop front during the twentieth century. Here the large display window, shop door and side doors are bracketed between slim fluted side columns, above which the moulded fascia extends across the building with scrolled-end brackets (Fig. 29). The upper-floor levels have pairs of Georgian windows equally spaced across the plain rendered elevation.

Fig. 28. The rendered house on Main Street Lower has a detailed shop front at ground level and Georgian windows on the upper floor. The replacement traditional shop front of the house and shop has a central doorway, display windows and a decorated and moulded fascia.

Fig. 29. The ends of the shop front of the premises on South Main Street have moulded timber side columns, scrolled-end brackets and a decorated fascia.

12. Corner House and Pub, Main Street Lower, Eighteenth Century

The corner house and pub is positioned at the junction of Main Street and Henrietta Street and unusually, features slate hanging on the two upper floors (Fig. 30). The house dates from the eighteenth century, is three storeys high, with a dormer window at attic level. The narrow gable end of the block faces onto Main Street and has had a traditional shop front at ground level. This has a timber double-pane display window and pub entrance door with narrow side columns and rendered panels on either side (Fig. 31). Overhead the fascia extends across the shop front and continues around the corner. Above this, the first- and second-floor levels have a pair of Georgian windows equally spaced across the slate-hung elevation, with the top window lower than the one below. Round the corner, the wide Henrietta Street elevation is rendered on the ground level with painted advertising panels, the fascia, and wall-hung slates on the upper floors. Unusually, the doorway to the upper floors of the house is positioned to one side of the Henrietta Street elevation (Fig. 32). Here the door is panelled with a plain rounded fanlight, and single standard Georgian sliding sash windows on the first and top floors – matching the window pattern of the Main Street elevation.

Fig. 30. The outstanding features of the three-storey house and pub at the corner of Main Street and Henrietta Street include the upper-floor wall slating and the box-framed shop front.

Fig. 31. The shop front of the house and pub on Main Street has a wide display window with the pub door to one side, set between rendered columns.

Fig. 32. The side entrance to the upper floors of the house and pub on Henrietta Street features a panelled door with a plain rounded fanlight, a moulded surround and a single Georgian window on each the two upper floors, directly above.

13. Church of St Iberius, Main Street North, *c.* 1766

The Church of St Iberius on Main Street dates from around 1766 and is one of the earliest Georgian public buildings completed in Wexford town. The original eighteenth-century street elevation featured a main symmetrical double-storey block with a projecting central bay. The building was set back from the street line and had a complex arrangement of side doors, Georgian windows and camber-headed windows, in addition to a pediment roof on the central bay (Fig. 33). This initial Main Street elevation was, however, given a more complex appearance around 1882 by the architect John Roberts when a new front porch was added and the original windows were replaced, and a decorated gate and railings were stretched across the front of the building (Fig. 34). The new three-storey porch was attached to the front of the projecting bay (Fig. 35). This included a cut-stone entrance archway, pointed double-opening Gothic-style windows on the two upper levels, a clock face on the upper level, and a roof-top cupola with a tall spire. The original Georgian windows of the main bays were replaced by arched Gothic-style examples with single and quadruple openings that featured sliding sashes, ogee arches, floral decorations, overhead relieving brick-cambered arches, and rounded sides arranged individually (Fig. 36) and in groups (Fig. 37). Internally the eighteenth-century interior of the church survives intact and is of exceptionally fine quality. The nave is rectangular in plan with a U-shaped upper-level gallery and a projecting curved organ loft, all supported by slim cast-iron columns. The altar table is positioned in a curved apse with an arcade of circular columns and arches separating it from the main body of the nave. The church also has a decorated curved altar rail, timber box pews, attractive plasterwork, rich stained-glass windows, and wall-mounted memorials.

Fig. 33. Sketch of the original Georgian elevation of the Church of St Iberius on Main Street North, from a painting on an upper window of the church.

Above left: Fig. 34. The elaborate amended elevation of the Church of St Iberius has individual and clustered Gothic-style windows, a three-storey entrance porch, and a cupola.

Above right: Fig. 35. The added front porch of the Church of St Iberius features the cut-stone entrance arch, rendered upper levels, Gothic-style windows, and a domed cupola.

Below left: Fig. 36. The individual Gothic Revival windows of the Church of St Iberius feature sliding sashes, ogee heads, decorated moulding, and coloured-brick overarches.

Below right: Fig. 37. The grouped windows of the Church of St Iberius are similarly arranged to the single windows with similar sliding sashes, ogee heads, decorated moulding, and coloured-brick overarches.

14. Former Market House, Corn Market, 1775

The former market house is a two-storey hipped-roofed building with a range of arched doors and window overlooking Corn Market (Fig. 38). The building was opened as a market house in 1775 and the open ground-floor space functioned as the trading area for the town's markets. During this period, the ground-floor arches were originally open, and spaced uniformly across the front to provide an open arcade to the market space. In 1849, the building was converted to a ballroom at which time the ground-level open space was filled in and doors and windows were inserted in the arcade. Later still, the building came into use as the Town Hall. The arches are unquestionably the most distinctive feature of the building. The two end arches of the ground-level arcade have timber-panelled doors and a fanlight (Fig. 39), while the intermediate arches have timber round-headed windows. Each of the semi-circular arcade arches has cut-stone surrounds and wedge-shaped arch stones. The five round-headed windows on the upper level are arranged directly above each of the arcade arches. These have timber Georgian-style sashes set into cut-stone arches and surrounds (Fig. 40). In 1974, the use of the building changed again when it became the home of the Wexford Arts Centre. Elements of the original structure, including the staircase and internal columns, remain intact.

Fig. 38. The position of the double-storey former market house, with its arched arcade, Georgian windows, quoins, string courses, and gabled roof, presents an impressive vista from Corn Market.

Fig. 39. The first-floor windows of the former market house have semi-circular arches with cut-stone block surrounds and wedge-shaped keystones.

Fig. 40. The panelled double door of the former market house is set into an arched opening with stepped cut-stone surrounds and a wedge-shaped keystone.

15. Terraced Town House, Abbey Street, 1800

The town house on Abbey Street forms part of a uniform streetscape of Georgian town houses that date from around 1800 (Fig. 41). The house is three storeys high, with a rendered elevation, three windows across the front, and a door case to one side. The standard Georgian up-and-down sliding sashes on the three floors are set in vertically proportioned openings with multiple gazing panes (Fig. 42). The top-floor windows are lower in height than those below, although the central window opening on this level is blank with sashes painted in – inserted perhaps to project an overall symmetrical balance. The arched door case has a panelled door set between rounded columns with carved heads, an elaborate diamond inscribed entablature, and a semi-circular fanlight (Fig. 43). Internally much of the original workmanship survives, including the plasterwork, stairs and doors.

Fig. 41. The terraced town house extends along part of the Abbey Street Georgian streetscape.

Left: Fig. 42. The windows of the terraced town house on Abbey Street have up-and-down sliding sashes with small panes.

Below: Fig. 43. The door case of the Abbey Street terraced house includes a moulded surround and a radial fanlight.

16. Corner House and Pub, Bull Ring, 1800

The corner house and pub is strategically positioned at the junction of the Bull Ring and North Main Street, with a splayed corner, giving it a three-street elevation (Fig. 44). The rendered block is three storeys high and dates from around 1800 with a shop front on the ground level and replacement windows on the two upper-floor levels. The shop front extends around the three street fronts, with a mixture of wide display windows, glazed panelled doors and a continuous fascia with painted signage. The corner splay (Fig. 45) and North Main Street elevation have single replacement vertically proportioned windows on each level, while the wider Bull Ring elevation has two similar windows on each level. Overhead the hipped-slated roof is partially hidden by a moulded parapet.

Fig. 44. The three-storey corner house and pub is strategically located on the corner of the Bull Ring and North Main Street with a three-sided elevation.

Fig. 45. The splayed front of the corner house and pub at the intersection of the Bull Ring and Main Street South has a wide shop front and door, an inscribed fascia and a single replacement window on each of the upper-floor levels.

17. Warehouse, Sinnott Place, 1800

The vast stone and brick-built warehouse on Sinnott Place has a run of twenty windows per floor extending in a uniform pattern along the street front (Fig. 46), while the much narrower gable end of the building has three windows per floor. The block dates from around 1800 and is six storeys in height with an additional half-gable roof storey. The partial stone and brick street elevation has a round-headed sheeted doorway at one end with a semi-circular fanlight over. The windows are slightly vertical in proportion with brick surrounds and camber arches, although the original window sashes have been replaced at some period (Fig. 47). The walling has been reinforced by a system of metal surface plates with internal cross ties and the block has a mixture of brick and stone quoins. The hipped gable has a central door flanked on either side by a single window as well as three windows on each of the upper levels, in addition to a pair of camber-arched windows on the half-gable level (Fig. 48). The gable door is similar to the Sinnott Place door with a curved fanlight set into a brick camber arch.

Left: Fig. 47. The windows of the Sinnott Place warehouse have brick surrounds, flat arched brick heads, multiple-pane replacement sashes, and metal surface plates.

Opposite left: Fig. 46. The vast stone and brick warehouse on Sinnott Place, with its rows of windows, is a splendid example of the survival of Wexford's industrial past.

Right: Fig. 48. The gable elevation of the Sinnott Place warehouse has a central doorway, brick-surrounded windows, mixed quoins, and a pair of cambered dormer-level windows.

18. Former Malt House, Peter Street, 1800

The former malt house is one of a number of eighteenth-century stone-built industrial buildings on Peter Street and dates from around 1800, when Peter Street was developing into a significant malting centre. The building reflects one aspect of Wexford's malting industry, where grain was converted to malt, first by soaking the grain in water, then allowing it to sprout and dry. Subsequently the malt was shipped to Dublin and used in the production of beer and whiskey. The small stone-built former Peter Street malt house is three storeys high with an attic storey and a replacement corrugated sheeted-metal roof. The gable faces onto the street, has brick quoins and a half gable at roof level. The elevation has a pair of windows on each side of the three floors, a door on the ground floor and a single louvered opening on the attic level. This was possibly a drying room (Fig. 49). The windows have brick cambered heads and stepped brick surrounds. The windows lack sills and have replacement sashes (Fig. 50). The window opening on the left-hand ground floor has been altered in the past and converted to a doorway opening onto the street.

Left: Fig. 49. The stone-built former malt house on Peter Street is three storeys high with an attic floor, and the entrance door and windows facing onto the street.

Above: Fig. 50. The rectangular camber-headed windows of the Peter Street former malt house have brick surrounds and brick cambered heads.

19. Mirrored House, Mary Street, 1815

The narrow fronted and rendered three-storey Georgian-style house on Mary Street is one of a matching pair of town houses. A unique feature of the house, as far as Wexford is concerned, is the duplicate mirror relationship between the elevation of the house and its immediate neighbour on the right-hand side (Fig. 51). A second unusual feature is the combination of the door and window into a single opening (Fig. 52). The low Georgian-style window has a pair of up-and-down sliding sashes with small panes that share a side frame with the panelled entrance door. Overhead both the first and second floors each have a single standard Georgian sash window – aligned one above the other, characteristically with the upper sash lower than the one below.

Left: Fig. 51. The street elevation of the house on Mary Street is an exact mirror Fig. of the three-storey house beside it: a unique feature in Wexford.

Above: Fig. 52. The combined sliding sash window and door of the Mary Street house is fitted into a single opening, as is the case with the adjoining house.

20. Former Malt House, Peter Street, *c.* 1825

The former stone-built industrial building is another former malt house on Peter Street. This is four storeys high and dates from around 1825. The street front elevation has a system of windows on all floors and block and start quoins at each end (Fig. 53). The windows are square with staggered brick surrounds and brick cambered-arched heads and metal louvers (Fig. 54). The left-hand end of the ground level has recently been renovated. The original windows have been blocked and that section of the masonry has been rendered. In addition, a doorway has been inserted as have five small fixed-pane windows. The return at the opposite end of the block has a wide sheeted door set into a cambered brick arch with brick surrounds and wide cambered casement sashes on each of the three upper levels (Fig. 55). The return also has a second door at first-floor level. This is reached by a flight of stone steps and metal railings that stretch across the front of the adjoining stone industrial building.

Fig. 53. The wide street elevation of the former malt house on Peter Street has six camber-headed windows on each of the four floors, with a small section of rendering and small fixed-cased windows at one end.

Above: Fig. 54. The camber-headed windows of the return elevation of the Peter Street former malt house have brick surrounds and brick-cambered heads.

Left: Fig. 55. The return elevation of the former malt house on Peter Street has a wide entrance door, cambered windows and a first-floor door reached by a flight of stone steps with a metal handrail.

21. Former Bank, Crescent Quay, 1832

The former Bank of Ireland building faces onto Crescent Quay and dates from 1832. The Georgian building was designed by the architect John Howard Louch in a symmetrical Palladian style in the manner of an Italian Renaissance palace. The building is, however, one of a number of Wexford bank buildings that underwent a change of use, when the building was converted to office use around the late twentieth century. Later, around 2003, the function changed once more when the building was converted into a pub and a curved extension was completed on the west end around 2007. The original block of the building has a central door case, flanked on either side by a Venetian window all set in rusticated stonework, while the plain cut-stone upper floors have three windows uniformly spaced across the front (Fig. 56). The panelled entrance door is set into a temple-style door case with rounded side columns, a moulded entablature, or cross piece, and a radial semi-circular fanlight above (Fig. 57). The door

Fig. 56. The elegant Palladian-style cut-stone elevation of the former bank building faces across Crescent Quay.

case is positioned in a semi-circular archway with wedge-shaped arch stones. The doorway is approached by four cut-stone steps with spear-headed metal handrails – that return across the front of the building. The flanking three-part Venetian windows on either side are divided into a wide central sliding sash and a slim side sash on either side. Each window has a plain cut-stone surround with a flat moulded pediment overhead. The timber first-floor windows have sliding sashes with twelve small panes, moulded cut-stone surrounds and overhead pediments. The top-floor windows, in contrast, are similar in style but lower in height and have no surrounds. In contrast to the Georgian character of the main block, the striking east-end extension, designed by Stephen Carr architect, is in the form of a segmental, or mushroom-shaped, structure that features ribbed-zinc cladding, a low cut-stone plinth and two doorways with pyramid hoods, in addition to an irregular pattern of small square windows (Fig. 58).

Above left: Fig. 57. The door case of the former bank building on Crescent Quay is in the form of a Classical temple with a panelled door, rounded side columns, a flat entablature, a semi-circular fanlight, a semi-circular surround, and spear-headed handrails.

Above right: Fig. 58. The intriguing half-circular and domed zinc-faced extension to side of the former bank building.

22. Harbour Office, Crescent Quay, 1838

The harbour office on Crescent Quay is another fine example of Wexford's Palladian architecture which dates from 1838. The architect of the office is uncertain, although the building has a distinct similarity to the nearby former bank building (Building 21) designed by John Louch. The double-storey symmetrical block has a central round-headed doorway with a round-headed window on either side and three Georgian windows at first-floor level, in addition to spear-headed cast-iron railings that stretch across the front (Fig. 59). The ground-level masonry is rusticated while the upper level is plain ashlar with a plain cut-stone string between the levels. The central doorway has a panelled door set between slim moulded columns. These have scrolled fluted brackets that support a plain entablature, or cross piece, above which is a semi-circular fanlight with radial-arranged glazing. The flanking Georgian win-

Fig. 59. The cut-stone double-storey symmetrical Palladian-style front of the harbour office faces across Crescent Quay.

dows with round-headed sashes have wide plain rendered surrounds set into the rusticated arch (Fig. 60). The three tall Georgian windows of the first floor are spaced evenly across the elevation, with a mix of triangular and plain moulded window pediments, above which a moulded parapet hides the slated roof. Inside the office building, some of the original joinery and plasterwork remains intact. Standing in the landscape open space on the estuary side of the Crescent is the memorial to Commodore John Barry of the American Revolutionary Navy (Fig. 61). The figure of Barry that looks out on Wexford harbour was unveiled in 1956 and was created by the American sculptor Wheeler Williams.

Above left: Fig. 60. The ground-floor Georgian windows of the harbour office have round-headed sashes and wide plain rendered surrounds set into the rusticated arch.

Above right: Fig. 61. The Wheeler Williams bronze memorial maritime figure looks out over Wexford harbour and commemorates Commodore John Barry of the American Revolutionary Navy.

23. Young Men's Christian Association Building, North Main Street, 1860

The Young Men's Christian Association (YMCA) building on North Main Street dates from 1860 and was designed by the architect Edwin Thomas Wills. The block was built as a social and community centre for young people in Wexford, but it was sold around 2000 and is now in commercial use. The two-storey building has a symmetrical brick elevation that fronts directly onto the street, with a coach arch to one side, a slightly projecting central bay and brick eaves (Fig. 62). The main feature of the elevation is the impressive cut-stone temple-style front entrance porch (Fig. 63). This has double doors flanked by half-round columns, with a moulded entablature and triangular moulded pediment. The Georgian-style sliding sash windows on each level have large glazing panes. The interior accommodation includes four large rooms at ground level, a large room on the upper level and a central staircase. Many of the significant original features of the building survive, including the staircase, joinery and decorative plasterwork.

Fig. 62. The former Young Men's Christian Association building on Main Street South features a brick elevation, a side coach arch, a temple-style porch and Georgian-style windows with large panes.

Fig. 63. The impressive entrance porch to the former Young Men's Christian Association building features a double door, half-round columns, a moulded entablature and a triangular pediment.

Victorian Wexford

1835–1914

24. Former Methodist Church Rowe Street Lower, 1835

The second half of the nineteenth century saw the emergence of a more Romantic approach to building in Wexford, as attempts were made to reintroduce past forms of architecture such as Gothic. This movement is known as Victorian, although Victorian and Georgian buildings frequently emerged side by side. In Wexford, the most common form of the Victorian style to appear was the Gothic Revival. This movement sought to imitate the Gothic ideals of the medieval period though the use of antique-based features including: heavy stone walling, steep gables, buttresses, slated roofs, towers, irregular plan forms, and pointed door and window openings. The former Methodist church in Rowe Street represents a typical example of a Gothic Revival style. It was built in 1835 and is one of the earliest Victorian buildings completed in Wexford. It stands at the corner of Rowe Street Lower and Mallin Street with the tall nave and attached side-entrance porch facing Rowe Street Lower (Fig. 64) and the end gable facing Mallin Street. The rendered nave walling is ruled and lined with five lancets, or tall slim windows, spaced regularly across the Rowe Street elevation, with long and short rendered quoins and a cut-stone date stone inscribed MDCCCXXXV (1835) over the central window (Fig. 65). The pointed arched lancets have Y-shaped tracery, Georgian sliding sashes and hood moulding (Fig. 66).

The single-storey entrance porch is also ruled and lined with the church door to one side, long and short quoins and a rose window on the street gable (Fig. 67). This has triangular panes and is set into a pointed arched niche. The nave has a small landscaped forecourt that is separated from the street by an arrow-tipped cast-iron railing and a double gate with decorated piers and a curved metal archway. The Mallin Street elevation is gabled with a pair of lancet windows, similar to those on the front, and a panelled door in a rectangular opening. The church went out of use around 1977 when the congregation merged with the Presbyterian congregation in Anne Street (Building 25), although the internal gallery, stairs and decorated plaster ceiling remain intact.

Opposite above: Fig. 64. The former Gothic Revival Methodist church on Rowe Street has lancet windows, long and short quoins, a projecting entrance porch and cast-iron gates and railings.

Opposite below: Fig. 65. The date stone of the former Methodist church over the central window of the Rowe Street elevation is inscribed: MDCCCXXXV (1835).

Right: Fig. 66. The arched lancet windows of the former Methodist church have Y-shaped tracery, Georgian sliding sashes and hood moulding.

Above: Fig. 67. The wooden rose window on the gable of the entrance porch to the former Methodist church on Rowe Street is set into an arched niche with a moulded surround and eight triangular panes.

25. United Presbyterian and Methodist Church, Anne Street, 1843

The church in Anne Street was designed by the architect Thomas Willis in the Gothic Revival style on an individual site. It opened as the Presbyterian church in 1843. In 1977, the community merged with the Wexford Methodist group and the name United Presbyterian and Methodist Church was adopted. The church is set back from the street front, has its gable to the front (Fig. 68) and an 1843 date stone. The steep impressive stone gable has a large high-level window with an arched doorway underneath and square buttresses at each corner. These have pinnacle heads, with an additional similar pinnacle on the apex of the gable. The Tudor arched entrance door is sheeted with a hood moulding and long and short side blocks (Fig. 69). The high-level Tudor-style window has timber Y-shaped tracery with cross-lattice glazing, long and short side blocks, and hood moulding (Fig. 70). The church forecourt is separated from the street by rendered piers and cast-iron gates. Internally the church has timber wainscoting around the walling, panelled pews and a timber pulpit.

Fig. 68. The rough stone gable street elevation of the United Presbyterian and Methodist Church on Anne Street has an arched doorway and window with square end buttresses topped by pointed pinnacles.

Fig. 69. The timber-sheeted door of the United Presbyterian and Methodist Church on Anne Street is set within a moulded Tudor arch.

Fig. 70. The large gable Tudor arched window of the United Presbyterian and Methodist Church on Anne Street has four panels, cross-lattice glazing and wooden Y-arranged tracery.

26. Former Granary, Charlotte Street, *c.* 1850

The three-storey former granary building on Charlotte Street is part of a uniform terraced streetscape and dates from around 1850. The rendered street front is ruled and lined with end quoins, cast-iron structural plates and has a uniform pattern of doors and windows on all three levels, including the central doors that are positioned one above the other on each level. These doors allowed goods to be raised and lowered to the upper levels directly from the roadside (Fig. 71). The ground level has a central timber-panelled double door with a fanlight set into a camber-arched opening, in addition to a pair of flat-headed side doors positioned on each side of the central door, each with a decorated wedge-shaped keystone. The first floor has a central doorway similar to the one immediately below (Fig. 72), in addition to a window on each side. These timber windows are Georgian in style with sliding sashes and multiple panes (Fig. 73), and have rendered wedge-shaped keystones. In contrast to the lower floors, the second-floor door has a plain flat-headed double door with a flanking Georgian window, similar to those on the first floor.

Fig. 71. The elevation of the three-storey terraced former grain store on Charlotte Street has a regular geometric arrangement of doors and windows on each level.

Fig. 72. The central doors of the former grain store on Charlotte Street are positioned one directly above the other on each level.

Fig. 73. The Georgian windows of the former grain store have up-and-down sliding sashes and a decorated wedge-shaped keystone above the head.

27. Church of the Immaculate Conception, John Street Lower, 1851

In 1850 it was decided at a public meeting in Wexford town that two Catholic parish churches – the Church of the Immaculate Conception and the Church of the Assumption – would be built. In a most unusual arrangement, the two churches were built to a similar identical design – the Church of the Immaculate Conception at the junction of John Street Lower and Rowe Street Upper and the twin structure on Saint Joseph Street (Fig. 74). Both of the churches were built outside the historic core, although the Church of the Immaculate Conception was positioned just beyond the line of the town wall and even today has a significant impact on the skyline of the historic core – and is consequently worth inclusion in this volume. Work started on the Church of the Immaculate Conception in 1851 in a Gothic Revival style to the design of the architect Richard Pierce and included a decorated cast-iron boundary railing. The five-stage gable entrance tower faces onto John Street Lower. It has stepped corner buttresses with figure sculptures at ground level, a central arched entrance door, a magnificent second-stage pointed east window with Y-shaped tracery and stained glass, a pair of pointed windows on the second and third levels, and a tall spire with a clock face underneath (Fig. 75). The side elevation of the church faces onto Rowe Street and includes a lean-to side aisle, entrance porch, and a sequence of pointed traceried windows at high level (Fig. 76). The interior of the church has an arcade of pointed arches that separate the tall central nave from the lean-to side aisles, pointed windows, tiled flooring, a timber-trussed and sheeted roof, and a magnificent stained-glass east window (Fig. 77).

Fig. 74. The twin churches of the Immaculate Conception and the Church of the Assumption share a range of common Gothic Revival features including a central nave, side aisles, a tall entrance tower, as well as pointed door and window openings.

Fig. 75. The four-level entrance tower of the Church of the Immaculate Conception faces onto John Street Lower and features an elaborate moulded entrance archway, pointed windows, stepped-corner buttresses, carved figures, and a tall spire.

Fig. 76. The Rowe Street side aisle of the Church of the Immaculate Conception features pointed windows on the ground and upper levels and a single-storey gabled side porch.

Fig. 77. The interior of the Church of the Immaculate Conception features low side aisles separated from the central nave by an arched arcade, with pointed windows, and a wooden sheeted roof.

28. Former Mechanics Institute, Main Street North, 1858

The Mechanics Institute building that dates from 1858 was one of several such institute buildings erected in Ireland during the nineteenth century, to act as a social and education club for working men. The Wexford building in Main Street North was designed by the architect Sir Edwin Thomas Willis and was blended into the terraced streetscape, where the accommodation included a library, a museum and a meeting room. The institute ceased to function during the twentieth century and for a period became the office of the *Wexford People* newspaper. The three-storey building has a double-arch entrance front at ground level and a pair of rendered upper storeys, although the building now has two independent retail uses (Fig. 78). The ground level of the building has a pair of segmented arches with replacement entrance screens, springing from hexagonal columns and with a moulded and framed fascia panel. This stretches across the width of the building and is inscribed in upper-case lettering with the title: 'MECHANICS INSTITUTE'. The two rendered upper floors of the building each have a pair of replacement Georgian windows. The lower windows are taller than the ones above and the two floor levels are separated by a continuous cut-stone string course. The roof-level parapet has a projected moulding, above which is a dormer storey with a wide attic window.

Opposite: Fig. 78. The ground level of the former Mechanics Institute on Main Street North features a double camber-arched shop front with an overhead inscriber fascia. Each of the arched openings features an entrance door and display window.

29. Former Church of St Selskar, Selskar Abbey, Temperance Row, 1862

In 1862 a Gothic Revival church was built within the Selskar Abbey site. This was designed by the architect John Semple, and was positioned abutting the east side of the medieval church tower (Building 1). The building was, however, dismantled in 1961 and only the stonework of the unroofed nave remains (Fig. 79). The ruin does, however, offer an interesting impression of the nineteenth-century Gothic Revival building process when the stone masons completed their work and left the site. Semple's church was laid out in a rectangular form with a narrow west-end porch that abutted the medieval tower and provided it with a new entrance. The nave walls of the surviving shell have an arrangement of narrow windows spaced between slim buttresses and tall gabled end buttresses (Fig. 80). The windows have pointed arched heads with hood mouldings and the buttresses are capped with pointed pinnacles. At the east end, the gable wall has a dynamic triple arrangement of tall pointed window openings, moulded eaves coping, and tall narrow niches cut into the face of the corner buttresses (Fig. 81).

Fig. 79. The roofless masonry structure is all that remains of the Gothic Revival Church of St Selskar in Selskar Abbey.

Fig. 80. The nave wall of the former Church of St Selskar features slim pointed window openings spaced between square buttresses.

Fig. 81. The east window of the former Church of St Selskar has a triple arrangement of arched openings with hood mouldings, flanked by tall corner buttresses.

30. Former Bank, Crescent Quay, 1864

The former National Bank on Crescent Quay is a late example of a Georgian-style palace-fronted building of exceptional quality. It was designed by the architect William Francis Caldbeck and dates from 1864. The cut-stone building is three storeys high with an elaborate symmetrical elevation that includes a slightly projecting entrance bay at either end, and sits within an extended waterfront terrace of largely twentieth-century buildings that face onto Wexford harbour (Fig. 82). The ground-floor level is rusticated with three semi-circular-headed, large-pane windows, spaced between the semi-circular temple-fronted doorways of the two end bays (Fig. 83). These have a panelled door and fanlight, set into a semi-circular opening including a wedged keystone, flanked with rounded side columns, and a moulded entablature or cross beam (Fig. 84). On the two upper-floor levels the five windows are spaced evenly across the elevation. The first-floor examples have cut-stone surrounds, a mixture of cambered, triangular and flat-pedimented heads, and large-pane sliding sashes. The second-floor windows are lower and less elaborate with cambered heads, above which the roofline is marked by a bracketed balustraded parapet.

Fig. 82. The former National Bank building sits into a long terrace of largely twentieth-century buildings on Crescent Quay that face onto Wexford harbour.

Fig. 83. The ground-floor level of the former bank building on Crescent Quay is rusticated with three semi-circular-headed, large-pane windows, spaced between the semi-circular temple-fronted doorways of the two end bays.

Fig. 84. The symmetrical palace-fronted former National Bank building has two projecting side entrance bays with arched door cases.

31. Market Building, Bull Ring Square, 1870

The Gothic Revival style market building on the Bull Ring Square was erected by Timothy O'Connor in 1870, in the form of two long single-storey parallel retail blocks spaced apart by a narrow pedestrian courtyard. The elevation facing onto the Bull Ring features a wrought railing with cut-stone piers that provide access to the courtyard, flanked on either side by the matching end gables of the retail blocks (Fig. 85). Each of the rendered gables is ruled and lined, has a decorated timber bargeboard with a timber final, rendered corner quoins, and a central Georgian window with stepped stone surrounds (Fig. 86). The windows are tripartite in form with a segmental head, a wide central sliding sash and narrow side sashes. Round the corner on Common Quay, the extended stone-side elevation has a continuous arcade of camber-headed square brick niches and a cut-stone continuous sill. The matching gables and entrance to the courtyard face onto the small landscaped Bull Ring Square, near the centre of which is a figure sculpture commemorating the 1798 Rebellion. The figure is mounted on a stepped pedestal, was the work of the notable sculptor Oliver Sheppard, and was unveiled in 1905 (Fig. 87).

Fig. 85. The side by side matching twin-faced double block of the market building faces onto the small Bull Ring Square.

Fig. 86. The rendered elevation of each of the matching market building gables features an intricate barge board and tripartite curve-headed Georgian window.

Fig. 87. The pedestal mounted bronze pike man on the Bull Ring Square celebrates Wexford's part in the 1798 Rebellion.

32. Commercial Premises Building, Commercial Quay, *c.* 1875

The commercial premises building on Commercial Quay is one of a pair that looks out over Wexford harbour, although the adjoining building has been altered and extended. The attractive rendered and painted mixed-use building dates from around 1875, is two storeys high and has a shop front at ground level that was added around 1825 (Fig. 88). The building probably acted as a house and came into use first as a Catholic club house in 1903 and later as the Young Men's Society Hall in 2018. Today the building is in commercial use. The finely detailed shop front has three panels separated by rendered framed uprights. The left panel has a glazed and panelled door. The central panel features three arched display sashes with lightly moulded framing and semi-circular heads, the right-hand rendered panel is largely blank with an advertising inscription. Overhead the decorated fascia extends across the full width of the elevation. The upper level of the building is rendered, ruled and lined and features a central casement window with small panes and a moulded surround. This is flanked on either side by a round-headed niche each with moulded surrounds and filled with a Classical urn. Overhead, the roof is screened by a deep moulded parapet.

Opposite: Fig. 88. The commercial premises building on Commercial Quay and the similar, but much altered, adjoining building facing onto Wexford harbour. The harbour front elevation of the commercial premises building on Commercial Quay has a pair of arched niches on the first-floor level that flank a framed central casement window.

33. Terraced House, Clifford Street, 1875

The two-storey terraced house is part of an extended terrace of thirteen houses that front onto Clifford Street and date from 1875 (Fig. 90). The terrace is set back and separated from the street front by a front garden and a low stone boundary wall, which follows the line of the town wall. The rendered, ruled and lined house front has a panelled door to one side with a square fanlight and moulded surround. The most distinguishing feature of the elevation is the Regency-style ground-floor window that includes timber sliding sashes with large panes, flanked on either side by timber shutters with diamond cut-outs (Fig. 91). Unusually, the open shutters are set into shallow recesses in the walling – the total configuration enclosed within a mounded surround. Overhead, the two first-floor windows are spaced evenly across the elevation. These, like the ground floor window, are vertically proportioned with moulded surrounds and up-and-down sliding window sashes with large panes.

Fig. 90. The two-storey rendered Regency terraced houses on Clifford Street have front gardens and stone front boundary walls built along the line of the medieval town wall.

Fig. 91. The main distinguishing feature of the house on Clifford Street is the Regency-styled window with timber sliding sashes and side shutters with diamond cut-outs.

34. Former Temperance Coffee House, Common Quay Street, 1877

The former Temperance Coffee House on Common Quay Street was, according the wall-mounted date stone, built in 1877 (Fig. 92). The building was inspired by the Wexford temperance movement of the nineteenth century and offered the facility for social gatherings free of the influence of alcohol. The imposing rendered gable-fronted building faces onto Common Quay, stands two storeys high, with a shop front at ground level, windows at first-floor level, and the circular rendered date stone in the triangular of the gable (Fig. 93). The shop front is divided into five openings by rendered pilasters, or uprights. The panelled door sits in the left-hand panel, while the remaining panels are filled by large replacement display windows. The deep, but plain overhead fascia has a moulded cornice and stretches across the full width of the building. The five first-floor replacement windows have moulded camber heads and wedge-shaped keystones. The five windows are visually linked together by a continuous cornice that stretches between the window heads, while a moulded parapet stretches along the sloping gable lines. Internally, much of the original decorative plasterwork, as well as the internal cast-iron columns, remain intact.

Opposite: Fig. 92. The 1877 round and rendered date stone is enclosed by a moulded surround and mounted on the gable of the former Temperance Coffee House on Common Quay Street.

Above: Fig. 93. The rendered front of the former Temperance Coffee House building faces onto Common Quay Street with a ground-level shop front, first-floor windows, date stone, and a pronounced triangular gable.

35. Corner House, George's Street Upper, 1877

The compact house on the corner of George's Street and Abbey Street was the birthplace of Robert Brennan in 1881. Brennan was the leader of the Wexford Volunteers who took over Enniscorthy during the 1916 Rebellion. Later, he was a co-founder of *The Irish Press* newspaper and was appointed as the first Free State Minister to the United States in 1934 (Fig. 94). The L-shaped house, on the otherwise three-storey terraced house streetscape, is two storeys high with a slated roof and extends around the corner into Abbey Street. The rendered George's Street elevation is ruled and lined with a central door case and a pair of windows on each floor level (Fig. 95). The panelled door with its semi-circular fan sash is enclosed by a moulded surround and a wedge-shaped keystone that features a human facial likeness (Fig. 96). The irregularly spaced replacement casement windows on both levels have moulded surrounds with corner shoulders. The Abbey Street elevation is plainer with a single replacement casement window on each level.

Fig. 94. Robert Brennan, with other members of the Wexford 1916 War of Independence Volunteers. Brennan is seated in the first row, second from the left.

Fig. 95. The two-storey corner house on George's Street Upper has an arched central door and replacement windows.

Fig. 96. The arched door case of the corner house has a wedge-shaped keystone, a moulded surround and a leaded radial fanlight.

36. Former Bank, Custom House Quay, 1881

The former Provisional Bank is one of a number of Wexford's Victorian buildings that incorporates a complex irregular arrangement of mixed elements and materials. The former bank building is positioned on the corner of Custom House Quay and Anne Street, with elevations on both streets. The building is three storeys high, dates from 1881 and was designed by the architect Sir Thomas Newenham Deane. The Custom House Quay elevation has an arched window arcade at ground level, a pair of joined windows at first-floor level, three individual windows on the top level and wide overhanging eaves with exposed timber brackets (Fig. 97). The largely cut-stone ground-level arched arcade has three large round-headed windows with a moulded balustrade underneath. The windows are set between cut-stone columns – the end ones slightly wider.

Fig. 97. The Custom House Quay elevation of the former Provisional Bank features a range of mixed elements and materials including arched- and square-headed windows, cut stonework, moulded balusters, brickwork, stone and brick string courses and overhanging eaves.

Over the arches, a cut-stone entablature, or cross beam, spans the full width of the building. The two upper floors of the block are brick-faced, with projecting end piers that follow the line of the ground-level end columns to the roof line. At mid-point in the brickwork is a pair of joined replacement windows enclosed by a moulded cut-stone surround. The top floor is similar except that it has three replacement windows. The Anne Street elevation is broadly similar with more brickwork on the ground level, in addition to the elegant corner entrance door case. This is set in the end bay near the Custom House Quay corner with cut-stone surrounds and a triangular pediment beneath a cut-stone arch (Fig. 98).

Fig. 98. The stylish Anne Street doorway to the former Provisional Bank features a panelled door, cut-stone moulded and bracketed surround, carved triangular pediment, cut-stone archway, and elaborate corner columns.

37. Semi-detached House, Crescent Quay, 1882

Although built well into the Victorian period, the semi-detached house on Crescent Quay is one of a pair of Georgian-styled houses built looking across Wexford's Circular Quay in 1882. The ground-floor elevation of the three-storey house is rendered, measured and lined, while the upper-floor levels are slate hung (Fig. 99). The ground-floor level has a plain central panelled door unadorned except for a low three-paned fanlight, flanked on either side by a single standard six pane Georgian timber sliding sash window with plain wooden shutters (Fig. 100). The latter add to the unusual elevation of the house. The upper-floor windows are unevenly spaced across the slated front. These are similar in character and form to the ground-floor windows, although they lack shutters and the top-floor sashes are lower in height than the lower levels. Overhead, both houses have a continuous hipped and slated roof.

Fig. 99. The fronts of the semi-detached houses on Crescent Quay are rendered and lined at ground level with slate hanging on the two upper-floor levels.

Fig. 100. The panelled central entrance door of the semi-detached house has a low three-pane fanlight with a shuttered Georgian-style window on either side.

38. Railway Station, Redmond Square, 1890

Towards the close of the nineteenth century, the Dublin, Wicklow and Wexford Railway marked the introduction of the railway to Wexford by building the detached station building that faced onto Redmond Square in 1890. The long symmetrical single-storey slated cottage-style building is rendered, measured and lined with slightly projecting end bays (Fig. 101). The entrance door in the centre of the wide middle bay is flanked on either side by a pair of Georgian-proportioned replacement sash windows. These are double-paned and framed by a rendered moulded surround. The two forward-facing end bays are gabled, each with a pair of joined replacement windows similar to those of the central bay windows but with a wedge-shaped keystone. Overhead, the gabled roofs have a decorated barge board with a slim metal finial on the crown. In 1891, the passenger platform on the far side of the station building was covered by a hipped glazed canopy. This featured decorated cast-iron columns, a glass roof and carried the name of the builder: Thompson Brothers (Fig. 103). Immediately outside the building is the small landscaped Redmond Square, in the centre of which is a tall square-based obelisk erected in 1867 to commemorate the contribution of the prominent political Redmond family to the historic development of Wexford town (Fig. 104).

Fig. 101. The wide symmetrical single-storey cottage-style railway station on Redmond Square, with a slated roof and brick chimney stacks.

Above: Fig. 103. The platform canopy of the railway station has a glazed hipped roof carried on metal framing and cast-iron columns, with the name of the builder, Thompson Brothers, and the date 1891.

Below left: Fig. 102. The projecting gable-fronted end bays of the railway station have a central double sash window, a decorated barge board and a metal finial on the apex of the gable.

Below right: Fig. 104. The cut-stone obelisk in the landscaped Redmond Square commemorates the involvement of the Redmond family in the history of Wexford town.

39. Office Building, Selskar Street, 1894

The double-storey domestic-scale office building fronting Selskar Street is positioned on a rectangular site enclosed on three sides by Selskar Street, George's Street Lower and Trimmers Lane West – a site that once held the town house of Beauchamp Bagnal, commander of the Wexford United Irishmen during the 1798 Rebellion. The building was designed by the architect Joseph Kelly Freeman in an Edwardian style, dates from 1894 and features a range of different elements including mixed brickwork, projecting bays, vertically proportioned windows, a cast-iron railing, and a slated hipped roof. The intricate elevations on George's Street Lower and Selskar Street include splayed and rectangular corner and end bays, vertical replacement sliding sash windows, a double band of yellow brick string courses, decorated yellow brick brackets at eaves level, and a date stone on the upper level of the Selskar Street elevation (Fig. 105). This features a rectangular stone with the date 1894 and a triangular head (Fig. 106). The door case on the Selskar Street end bay has a panelled door with a semi-circular fanlight, set in a brick arch with an overhead stone hood moulding and keystone (Fig. 107). An unusual aspect of the building is the three-storey extension added to the Trimmers Lane West end of the block around 2005. This is minimalist in style with a full height glazed panel entrance and flat roof, which contrasts with the scale and brickwork of the original Freeman structure, as well as a glazed shop front on Trimmers Lane West with large horizontal windows on the two upper-floor levels. Immediately beside the office building is a fine bronze sculpture of the Wexford hurler, Nicky Rackard, created by the sculptor Mark Richards in 2012 (Fig. 108).

Fig. 105. The Selskar Street elevation of the office building on Selskar Street includes red and yellow brickwork, projecting corner bays, and a tall fully glazed corner entrance.

Above: Fig. 106. The first-floor date stone mounted on the Selskar Street face of the office building includes the cut-stone triangular block inscribed with the date: 1894

Below left: Fig. 107. The Selskar Street door case of the office building features a panelled door, semi-circular fanlight, brick arch, and a moulded cut-stone hood, keystone and metal railings.

Below right: Fig. 108. The bronze memorial of the Wexford hurler Nicky Rackard adjacent to the office building on Selskar Street.

40. Post Office, Anne Street, 1894

The Post Office building on Anne Street was, according to the first-floor level date stone, built in 1894. It was designed in a restrained Edwardian brick-fronted style by the Office of Public Works (Fig. 109), although, according to a later date stone, the building was refurbished in 1987. The building is three storeys high and features an arcaded shop front at ground level with rectangular windows on the first- and second-floor levels (Fig. 110). The shop front arcade features a stretch of four semi-circular arches. The three arches on the left side of the elevation have round-headed replacement sashes set into the arched openings with brick keystones and a continuous stone sill. The fourth arch on the right-hand side acts as the entrance. This has a double-panelled door with a cambered arch immediately above and a half-round fanlight higher up that matches those of the three window sashes. Immediately above the arcade, a brick-moulded cornice extends across the shop front. Higher up, the first-floor windows are evenly spaced across the elevation. These are vertically proportioned with camber heads, brick hood mouldings and large-pane replacement windows. The top-floor windows are similar, although a little lower in height, with square heads and continuous brick hood moulding. Immediately overhead, the roof parapet is formed by a double-moulded cornice and stretches across the front of the building.

Fig. 109. The framed 1894 terracotta date stone of Anne Street post office is positioned in the centre of the first-floor level above the brick fascia.

Fig. 110. The brick street elevation of the Anne Street post office features an arcaded shop front, with large-pane window sashes, and a double-moulded brick parapet.

Twentieth and Twenty-First Century Wexford

1899–2012

41. House and Shop, Main Street South, 1900

The shop and house on South Main Street is one of an identical pair of semi-detached buildings in the street terrace. The double-storey building was erected by Mary O'Connor around 1900 in a restrained Edwardian style featuring a mixture of red-coloured brickwork and yellow brick dressing to the windows (Fig. 111). The box-framed shop front is divided into four sections by plain uprights. The door to the upper floors is on one side, the shop door and large display windows are on the other side. Overhead, the fascia extends across the front of the building with scrolled-end brackets, a moulded top and the painted lettering of the shop sign. The replacement first-floor sliding sash windows have large panes, mixed red and yellow brick jambs, as well as mixed red and yellow brick camber arches (Fig. 112). The top-floor windows are similar except for the flat window heads. The roofline is marked by a yellow string course and a projecting brick roof cornice.

Fig. 111. The three-storey house on South Main Street has a box-framed shop front, mixed brick upper floors and vertically proportioned upper-level windows.

Fig. 112. The first-floor sliding windows of the three-storey house on South Main Street have mixed red and yellow brick jambs, cambered arches and brick hoods.

42. Dormer Cottage, Slaney Street, 1917

The dormer cottage is one of a terrace of four laid out along Slaney Street around 1917, several of which survive. The rendered elevation is ruled and lined and has a slated roof with a single half-dormer window (Fig. 113). This is the main aspect of the building and features a small eight-paned Georgian-style sliding sash window set into the triangular gabled half dormer. The ground level has a similar eight-paned window and a doorway to one side. This has a flat-headed panelled wooden door with a moulded surround and a wedge-shaped keystone (Fig. 114). An unusual feature here is the flat pediment hood immediately above the keystone that stretches across the width of the door opening.

Fig. 113. The attractive terraced dormer cottage on Slaney Street has a single Georgian window on each floor and a framed and moulded door case to one side.

Fig. 114. The panelled hall door of the dormer cottage has a moulded surround, a keystone and an overhead hood pediment.

43. Former Bakery, Main Street North, 1918

The intriguing three-storey former bakery building on Main Street North was built by Francis O'Connor in 1918 in a Dutch Gabled Revival style (Fig. 115), although this seems to be a rebuild and adoption of an earlier structure, as a mosaic panel at the entrance floor states that the building was established by Mr and Mrs M.J. O'Connor in 1860. The bakery was closed in 1979 and today is in retail use. The street elevation consists essentially of complex double-fronted gabled premises, which feature a ground-floor shop front and two upper floors. The shop front has a recently installed series of large full-size glazed panels with a recessed double shop door and a door to the upper levels at one side. The overhead moulded fascia has a central cambered

Fig. 115. The street frontage of the double Dutch gabled building on Main Street North has a wide shop front, rendered upper levels and curved Dutch gables.

panel and scrolled brackets at either end. The rendered and rusticated first-floor level has six Georgian-proportioned sliding windows spread across the front and a central projecting panel inscribed with the initials: FOC (Francis O'Connor) in the rustication between the windows. Immediately above the windows is an extended framed panel with capitalised lettering that reads: BREAD IS STILL THE STAFF OF LIFE – highlighting the former bakery use (Fig. 116). The plain rendered and lined upper-floor levels have four similar windows with moulded surrounds and a pair of double-curved Dutch gabled parapets. Overhead, the two side-by-side Dutch gables are the outstanding feature of the building, each with double curves and a flat head crowned by a ball-type finial.

Fig. 116. The first-floor level of the former bakery building features ruled and lined rendering, a plaque with the initials FOC, and a panel that reads: BREAD IS STILL THE STAFF OF LIFE.

44. Bank Building, Main Street, 1923

The Allied Irish Bank building on Main Street was opened as the 'Munster and Leinster Bank' in 1923 to the design of the architect Thomas Scally in a symmetric Palladian style. The granite four-storey over basement block was set back a little from the footpath to form a shallow paved front patio (Fig. 117). In its original form, the rusticated ground-floor level had three round-head windows with a round-headed entrance doorway to one side. Overhead, the three upper levels have a regular pattern of replacement windows with cut-stone moulded surrounds. All are vertically proportioned except the top level where the shorter examples have rounded heads. The upper levels also have decorated string courses and a corniced parapet. The ground level of the bank was, however, recently amended. The windows were replaced with alternative sashes, the doorway converted to a window and the window in the far side of the front was reduced in height (Fig. 118). During the same period, a new entrance porch was added to the left-hand side of the block. This featured cut-stone side walls and a semi-circular metal glazed roof (Fig. 119). This now provided access to a side entrance to the original block and to a later double-storey bank extension. In addition, a cut-stone fascia was extended over the round-headed window openings, while internally much of the original decorative work remains intact.

Fig. 117. The four-storey cut-stone bank building on Main Street has a landscaped patio between the front elevation and the edge of the footpath.

Fig. 118. The window openings of the bank building on Main Street have cut-stone surrounds and are aligned vertically and horizontally across the elevation.

Fig. 119. The recently established side entrance porch of the bank building on Main Street has cut-stone sides and a semi-circular glazed roof.

45. Town Library, Mallin Street, 2012

Wexford Town Library building on the corner of Mallin Street and John's Gate Street was developed by Wexford County Council around 2012 in a hi-tech style of architecture that is characterised by the use of a jagged outline, expressive steelwork and panelled glazing (Fig. 120). The three-storey central bay features extensive full-height glazed panelling that allows light into the building and allows views into the dramatic interior spaces of the library. Immediately in front of the glazing is a row of slim circular steel columns that extend upwards to the underside of the continuous steel parapet (Fig. 121). The southern end bay has a pattern of slit windows on three levels set in vertically arranged stone panels (Fig. 122). The end corner bay is single-storeyed and stepped back from the main building line, with the projecting entrance porch of the library at the inner corner junction. The junction of the three- and single-storey bay buildings share a mixed arrangement of full-height glazing and polished stonework panels. Internally the library features a hi-tech arrangement of vibrant open, mixed and split-level spaces (Fig. 123).

Fig. 120. The vibrant and expressive hi-tech form of the Wexford Library building extends along the edge of Mallin Street.

Fig. 121. The central bay of the Wexford Town Library features an extensive stretch of full-height glazing and metal columns through which the interior of the library can be viewed from the street.

Fig. 122. The southern bay of the library features polished stone cladding and a pattern of slit windows.

Fig. 123. The interior arrangement of the Wexford Town Library has an arrangement of large split-level public accommodation and intimate administrative spaces.